The Mask

poetry

Terry Watada

MAWEN⟨I
HOUSE

We acknowledge the support of the Canada Council for the Arts for our publishing program. We also acknowledge support from the Government of Ontario through the Ontario Arts Council, and the support of the Government of Canada through the Canada Book Fund.

Cover design by Sabrina Pignataro
Cover photo: TumOng / Kabuki, the mask Kabuki is a classical Japanese dance drama with theater form, which originated in the Edo period at the beginning of 17 century and was particularly popular among townspeople. / Shutterstock
Image on page 117: kvap / Japanese Traditional Face Mask stock photo/ iStockphoto

Library and Archives Canada Cataloguing in Publication

Title: The mask : poetry / Terry Watada.
Names: Watada, Terry, 1951- author.
Description: Includes bibliographical references and index.
Identifiers: Canadiana (print) 20230553664 | Canadiana (ebook) 20230553680 | ISBN 9781774151129 (softcover) | ISBN 9781774151136 (EPUB) | ISBN 9781774151143 (PDF)
Subjects: LCGFT: Poetry.
Classification: LCC PS8595.A79 M37 2023 | DDC C811/.54—dc23

Printed and bound in Canada by Coach House Printing

Mawenzi House Publishers Ltd.
39 Woburn Avenue (B)
Toronto, Ontario M5M 1K5
Canada
www.mawenzihouse.com

for bill, mike and jim

Contents

The Mask

Masks

In
    this august time   of
  festival   when warm

breezes caress and
humidity
        embraces

the
    season of *Obon*,

there is no music
that
    vibrates
  the air

no shrill whine of *fue*,
no thump
     of
        taiko

no *odori* choreography.
the
  girls and women
 stay at home

no food aromas
that entice   the throngs
to come and laugh and
sing and shout

no smoke to rise

and
      envelop,
   to permeate clothes,

but there are masks
that
      cover and uncover
    the true self.

in the dark night,
i slide
     along the linoleum floor
     of the house, checkered
     and newly waxed,
     where
          i was born and raised.

in front of me
     my father
in a summer *kimono*,
white
     and gleaming,
     his arms swinging

in practised movements,
his body   moving forward to
a silent rhythm

he turns and
     his *tengu* mask
gleams in the darkness
of stray light:

he protects the sacred forests and mountains.

mother sways behind him,
also
     in a summer *kimono*
     of *sakura* blossoms

with a diamond fan and
red clackers

she wears the mask
of a   *noh*
yomesan—white smooth skin,
tight eyes
red lips and black teeth

a beautiful, demure woman
moving to a silent
tanko
        bushi

and I wear the *kitsune*
the   mask of a fox.

I want to be playful,
to celebrate,
to honour, and dance
the *awa odori*,

but I cannot.

instead, I reach for my parents
and they
                turn,
        crack and disintegrate

disappear
like so much dust in a storm

and I hear the buzz, smell
the antiseptic and feel the
pain of a hospital
and I can do nothing but cry out.

5

my mask falls:
      strangers and
    relatives walk by

wearing
the   mask of *oni* and *hannya,*
their
      horns shaking
    with their cackling.

The Haunting

The Haunting

... begins
        with
    the rain

at night
    when I am in
  my parents' bed-
room   gazing
through
    the dripping
glass
at the empty world.

no lights,
only the aroma
of
    incense
and the sound of
a humming bell.

the Buddha is near; the Buddha is always near.

I can't see the rain
I can't
    feel the rain
I can't taste the rain

I
  can
only hear the rain

hitting the window
panes,
         shadows of
ghosts visiting.

And my mouth gapes open in awe.

Dreams

there was a time   when
i
    walked
hand in hand   with dad
in
    a blizzard

the snow and ice
covered us until i couldn't
see
    him anymore   but

i knew he was with me.
his hand,
    warm, strong, and big,
held tight,

a lifeline in the dream
of
    a storm.

wish I could feel that grip again,
even
     for a minute.
  I would know I was headed
  for home.

stays with me
like the redolence of that dream.

and then I held his thin hand
as
      he looked up at me
from his wheel-
chair

and told me of his dream
of
running, dragging
the wind behind him;

i
   could only smile
at the tears
in his
mucus rimmed eyes

and i closed mine,   knowing
he will let go
        when
the blizzard   returns.

Ghost Scream

I hear his scream
in
    my sleep   it
wakes me in a cold sweat

the scream is full
of terror, mucus and
bile

I leap out of bed
and rush
down
     the darkened
   hall   but
then   I recall

I'm alone   no one
home.
    not in so many
   years.

when i was a kid,
on
    the cusp of
my teen years,
i heard Dad screaming,
waking the dead . . . in his
nightmare.

i ran down the hall
to
    his bedroom.
he was chuckling by
then,
didn't seem to bother
mom though the scream
had startled
her
    awake.

he was back in the truck
tumbling
            down
    the mountainside

sliding & crumbling in
turmoil

never ending   then and now
the crush &
        smash of ruin:
broken tree trunks, landslides of
    twisted vehicle parts   bashed-in
truck roof   pinched,
torn, bodies shredded

ever-
        green
    branches and needles

until it

stopped.   truck wedged
between twin rocks   jutting out
from the mountain.

back in the fall of '43,
        during the time
of war.   & imprison-
ment

lost one man that day,
Minamide,
the one who sat
 beside dad,
who writhed in the pain
of a crushed rib cage.

i rubbed
        his shoulders, reassuring
    him all was well.

he looked at me   with
kind eyes and patted
my hand.

And all was well.

the darkness
        closes around me
    and he is gone.

there's no one left
who remembers that crash.
not dad,
mom,   no relatives,
nor friends   or contemporaries

no one left.

I just have
the ghost scream to wake me,
to remind me with a nightmare
of
        my own,

and no   one to pat my hand
to reassure
        me that all
    is well.

Visions of Chisato

the clothesline   stretches
across the length
of the   backyard

proof of father's handiwork

and
white bedsheets shiver
in   the
      near-winter
wind.

but there is the promise of
sun
      light
   bright, warm & life-affirming

on laundryday   every Saturday

mom stands on a
platform   built by dad
and hangs the clothes
with
         homemade clothespins

to save money

but what was she thinking?
about
      girlhood
   in Japan   with sisters
   and brothers

and handsome parents
prospering   on
rice, fish, and lumber

or was she thinking
about her life
in
        Celestial Canada

where she
landed
        into struggle
    & poverty

on a lumber raft shack
floating   beyond
civilization

worried for
her baby son drowning
in
        the cold blue
    waters

of the Strait of Georgia

I see her dancing
among
                the white cotton
        sheets

arms led by pointed hands
curving round her body
as her legs strain
to
     gently perfect the choreography

an *odori* of joy
in   the cold air,
the rushing wind,
the light rain

her hair   grows wet
but
     she doesn't care

the past is behind her
the hate is behind her
the promise of
prosperity,
shining in her two sons' eyes

the spit of race, the rush of unintelligible words,
the rough, callused hands
grabbing, pushing,   and tightly gripping.

the rage of the mind
the tears
            of alien woods
    the fear of the uncertain
    in the fire of the
    endless,

but she survived

only to scrape
and live in a prairie shack   until . . .

I see her
lying in the grass,
her
        back to me

sitting up   her arms extended
for support   her hands planted
at a crooked angle
                and gazing
at a distant clothesline,
warm bedsheets   flapping &
beckoning   calling
her home, a 2-storey
                sagging house,

standing on the horizon,
a
        little weather-worn
        but standing.

she is young, a loose
summer dress,
    her hair done in a bun,
I can't see her face, but
I feel
    she is smiling.

she returns to our backyard,
hanging sheets
in the winter   of
her life and home.

a vision
    of Chisato
   soon fades into
   a world empty of her

and I am left with the snapping
of laundry   in the stiffening

wind,

but there remains
an aroma of fresh, clean
and inviting bedsheets.   the
aroma

        of a ghost.

A Photograph of Ghosts

flash
        of
the past – a near rhyme

light & moments

a flash that brings back
a flood
        of memory

hideki and me
standing
              in our backyard
        in about 1960,

I'm about half his height.   [a towering figure]

I must've been ten or thereabouts,
which
would make him 28.

he is young & strong
handsome, large face with a broad smile
his head   crooked just so   towards me
as if to say he was aware of our
height disparity,   and those glasses,
bought from an Eaton's catalogue back
in camp days, from 1942.   [when he was
10]

so happy he could see,

he danced around the schoolroom cabin
while classmates laughed at him.

his plaid shirt under
a sweater,
        strange,
    since it must've been July

I have on
the same shirt, similar if not the same
(which
        says a lot)
and holding   my brand-new Kodak camera

my dad, excuse me,
our dad bought it for me
on my birthday.

I too smiled
    I could take pictures
  like him . . . like

hideki

but no one taught me
how to   operate it
so, when I ruined
the first roll of film,

hideki slammed it
to the floor,
calling me "stupid" in
that moment.   wasted money,
the film and the camera

his face glowed red,
his
      glasses slipped
   down his nose from
   perspiration.

I said nothing . . . I lowered
my gaze
      and felt my body
    quake, drain

yet, I remember his arm around
my shoulder in the photo   I can feel its warmth,
love, comfort, and protection,
and I loved him, I wished to be like him;
for him to be proud of me.

not sure he ever was.

Yes, a photograph,
a flash
           of
the past – a near rhyme

like my brother and me.

Hideki and me
circa 1963
photo by Matsujiro Watada

Dust

My eyes
        are
    filled with dust

but not sleep
or
flaking wallpaper

night dust
made of dreams
and
        random thoughts.

a girl   permed hair
curls
        of blonde hair
    and skin,

and summer dress,
all alone   walking
a dirt road
        to school,

bright red   lipstick,
red high-heel shoes
covered
            in dust,
        she struggled to
        stay   upright.

(my brother's memory)

the image
      caked my eyes.

Cat in the Middle of the Road

a grey cat
    feral cat
  standing

(native to the
woods & mountains
surrounding a 1944
internment ghostcamp.

pine tar
on its moulting fur,
cockeyed and
limping)

in the middle of the dirt road,
bright eyes blazing at
a
    truck about
  to leave in moonlight;

it begins its chase
as
    the truck kicks
up dust in
its wake

the cat tries
to
catch up;
its eyes blazing
        fury.

but the dust clouds fold in,
the evening darkness
envelops   like smoke from
a fire

my brother's last
memory as he passes
into
        Nirvana.

A Frozen Forest

a poem for Bunji

as you walk
in
    a frozen forest,
look at the ice branches
around you

appreciate the
ice   glistening
  in the noonday
    sun,

and think of me,
smile and
    keep me warm in
    your heart

I watched you grow,
picked you up   when
you
    stumbled and fell.

I watched you shine
with
    achievement,
  so proud.

I watched   you double-over
in sorrow   when
you failed,

I
    tried to comfort.

i hope i did.

walk
      on the ice,
    listen to the crack
    and laugh my laugh.

smile and keep me warm in your heart.

Clouds in my Coffee

clouds in
    my coffee
  reflect the sky

no blue   just bright, sparkling rain,
    like falling
  sugar

      to the sea   to the sea
      to the open arms of the sea
      – so the old song goes.

summer:
when   we trod the beaches and sang
to
      the beach boys
and gazed at girls in bikinis

autumn:
when   the moon shadows sang
softly
      while stars winked
and sparked in my girl's eyes

but it was a time
when I saw with the
white
      of my eyes

now sadness
lies
      in the shadows

as I drink in
the clouds only to look up
to stop the tears
from
        falling
for I am alone tonight.

every night
like a prisoner
or a dying   patient.

she is gone   *to*
the
        sea to
    the sea.

all I can do is keep my head high and
whistle the refrain
        of a simple, old
    sad song.

ue o muite arukō
so
    my tear wells
    will not drain

into vacant streets.

The Devil's Hour

in
    the house
plays the music
that
        no one hears
    anymore,

and conversations
that
    took place
are no more.   Just empty
voices echoing
        in rooms contained by
        walls & ceilings.

from the lone dead
of midnight   to the
middle of the
Devil's Hour   I listen
to the
        lonely songs,
    the echoing conversations
    of longago,

and the loneliness of
the solitary beating heart

the quiet chaos
of the past   seeping
out into   stale,
cold air   vibrating –

memories sweep
through
            my being:

what was will never be again.

A Song,
    A Conversation,
    Alone

Summer Stars

Summer Stars

StarLight
        trickles
                down &
coats the glistening
barbed wire in the
muted
        summer
    night (

in the woods
silent
        for a 1000 years

canadian   prisoners
bleed
        memories of
    the lost
    streets, laughter and
    rain of Vancouver,

    the waterfront – distant
    breezes
    whispers of times past

    a lump
    in the throat, an ache
    in the body.

the stars
shine brightly,
un-
    aware of pain
    & loss.

but I feel the prickly heat
of the summer   beneath
those
        very same stars   (

80 years later)

it scrapes across my skin
like
        barbed wire.

it heats the blood
with
        the sting of
    injustice

it squeezes the eyes
with
        tears of shame
        and salt.

the forested trees
hold
        their prisoners,
reduced to their
elements in

the Precambrian
shield   a land-
scape of
    anonymous
  dead.

below the stars,
the empty and invisible
          still whisper
of their   loss
of
     home and
  kin

as they strain to pull on the haunted
and blank
faces
        of ghosts
      & spirits.

Summer stars:

the woods
        silently
absorb the light.

for Midori Iwasaki

Dragon Smoke

dragon
      smoke curls
   into
         the air

of *Celestial Canada*

as I   walk,
shedding
      memories
under-   neath
clearblue   skies,
I gaze in wonder
at
   the heavens

mama   dad
friends &
       relatives
   joyous gatherings,
   birthdays, anniversaries
   graduations, festivals . . .
   of likeminded friends around
   a dinnertable

   times past,
times
      gone.

white clouds wounded
by the black scar of
dragon
        smoke
expands   and spreads
across
        the horizon,
a rumble of thunder
and the rains come.

the tears of
dragon
        smoke

(*as Jim once
        called it)*

fall,
like the past, absorbed
by
        the ground,

to disappear . . .

The Burden

the
		burden
	of time weighs
	heavily
				on
			me.

night conjures
			images
		of parents, friends,
		brother

a childhood
spent
		in pain,
		shame

from hideki who couldn't live
with himself.

a lashing out   alienation
drove me to loneliness

to mike, bill, jim
a trio of support,
friendship   and care
long
		gone.

so, I am
alone   and
crying in my dreams

but my eyes are dry
in
     the dark
    wakefulness

shadows of a brother's grave,
the comfort of
my parents' resting place;
the
     empty image
    of ghosts.

sorrow changes its mask
but   the burden
     is always with me,
prolonged and murmuring . . .

The House of Genyo

Haunted by the Immaterial World

Genyo-no ie,
        the House of
Genyo

my mother's house
in
        Mihama, Japan,

    above
                a deep
    and slow-moving waterway,
    a tributary   of the Mimi River,
    that flows to the sea,

a sea of jellyfish and whales.

the house   at the top
of a long, meandering
road   is hidden

behind
a wall of barns full of
farm machinery
and
        storage bins

the arched
entrance   leads
to a courtyard
wide
        and dusty

a large estate
of *shoji*,
    flickering lights and
  polished floors and
  tatami

a concrete cooking area
with wood-burning stove,
a hand pump for water
and
    large *ofuro*
for nighttime bathing.

And at its heart is the
Genyo-*no Oba*

my mother's sister-in-law,
ancient
       and kind
   (my aunt

her husband long gone,
maybe died
    in the war
    maybe his younger brother   too.

(another uncle.

I wish
    I had known
   them.

makes me lonely somehow)

Genyo-*no Oba*
    cackled deep in
the estate   echoes of
madness.

But my aunts were alive,
when I visited back
in '59:

Hikosuke, ancient as well
and stern;
        Jo-mon,
    serious   no-nonsense,

her name sounded like
"German" to me.
and the third whose
name may have been
Kamu,   she
    gave me Japanese candy
  and kindness.

my favourite

I have a vivid
memory   of the four
dressed in black *kimono*
standing in a line, as if in
a photograph, while
mist
        surrounded them
  and swallowed

    them.

a shadow
        of the grave:
the youngest   sister,
absent from   the photo,
she remains translucent
            in the
mist,

a child who drowned
in the Mimi River
so
        long ago

she walks the halls of Genyo,
I
        believe.

my mother   felt
her presence,
standing as she did
            on warm
    tatami
                floors
in the middle of the
foyer to the other
rooms   of the house.

She stood
        shaking
    and crying

a pool of sorrow beneath
her vulnerable feet.

I wanted
        to hold her,
    comfort her,
    to
        console her.

I tried,
but   could not.

I was only 7.

and there was the stone *samurai*
in
    the garden outside
  a sideroom

a fierce face, his sword and
strength
            protecting us
and all past generations.

somewhere water gurgled
in
    the garden
bringing peace as we sat
in *seiza.*

and we
visited graves   in
adjacent hills

wooden staves
for markers   strange lettering
told of past lives, of strangers
& relatives
    incense burning constantly,
the
        clouds drifting like ghosts,
the scent their calling card.
the *bonsan*
chanted

        the *sutras*
        in an ancient raspy voice
        full of
        dust & charred remains,

and I was told the story
of grandpa, (another one I never
met)
gathering his children
before him and the *samurai*
and

    telling them of
his coming death.   no health
issues, no visible signs
of disease, no prediction of
accident,

just death at a precise moment
in time.

they all laughed,
I'm sure Kamu-*no Obaachan*
was the loudest.

yet *Ojiichan*
did
    die at the predicted
  time and day.

strange, I have
lived
     that same story
   ever since.

villagers say I bear
a striking resemblance
to him.
       yet I have had
     no such premonition.

maybe one day

I wandered the halls
of Genyo, so many
decades ago,
        the haunted halls,
        of Genyo.

the darkness
        surrounded
    and
        engulfed me,

but I felt safe.

I instead walk
through my ancestors'
thinning
            shroud of trans-
        lucence

and cry for my mother
in
        the waves of incense and
chanting of

the *Heart Sutra*
at
        her funeral.

The *Samurai*

In the
     garden
of nirvanic
peace,

the *samurai*
stands
     brooding,
scowling,
katana raised,

guarding, protecting:

eyes forever
sharp and glaring

threatening

arm muscles clenched,
leg
    muscles flexed,
  ready to
     do battle.

With who, with what, with . . .

the devils
that clatter across
the ceiling   at night

"mice," my mother says,
  but
    I'm not so sure.

the *oba*
that
    haunts the shadow'd
  halls   looking
  for lost family.

the ancestors
who rise in the smoke
out from
    the *butsudan*
to reclaim   *Genyo-no Ie*

their footfalls
squeak
     on nightingale
   floors

all haunting long.

no, so
I sit in a *samurai's* presence
seeking
    compassion
  in its
     cold stone heart
  (finding none)

  yet comforted by
  its strength,

a memory of childhood.

Fireflies

fireflies
        in
the cool darkness
of the garden   out-
    side the *House*
   of Genyo.

the stone *samurai*
stands on guard as the
dots of light fly, swoop
and curl, swirl about.

my mother said
they
      were the souls
  of my grandparents, uncles,
  aunts and cousins.

a moment of magic and wonder
to a seven-year-old   with-
in the haunted   *Genyo-no-ie.*

and now the fireflies
swarm
     and gather again
  on a humid, hot
  summer night

in Canada
to say
        hello to me, once
    more.

gentle, fleeting.   pinpoint
lights of beauty
as they drink on the tears
of
    longago days.

The *House of Genyo*: The Fall

standing
      at the
bottom
      of the sky,
a house, a home,
small and   luminous

soon
      crushed
by layers of dark
and storm

an *Oba* blessed with insanity
lit the stove   to cook for
missing
            family.

Genyo-no Oba, the *Old Lady of Genyo*,

she caught on fire   her cloth, grease-stained
sleeve flared   like a roman candle,
and
      she screamed and set other things ablaze
      in a panic.

as she kindled, her
cackle filled the house
with
      laughter turned
  to horror

fire – the dance of colour
between
    light and shadows   between

    ghost and being, the substance of
    being;
    between . . . life & darkness

*

the history of great-
grandfather   adopting
grandfather from a
bishop's family

the image of grandfather
working
        the land
in Mihama   building
the house at the top
of a promontory
overlooking a village
by
        the sea,

of grandfather
        marrying
        grandmother

with the promise
of prosperity &

the dream of seven children,
two older boys,
        five girls.

And then
the nightmare
of one   the youngest
drowning in the Mina
River.

they cried for days,
for
      the lost soul.

My *okaa*   left
family to be with
a
      lumberjack in the
wilds of BC.

the others married well and stayed in Japan.

The memory of
a demure,
young   girl of sixteen
            when she
married a tall young man,
strong with keen eyes
and conviction
in his soul.   Genyo Takehara
was
    the eldest son of
Iwakichi, a successful
entrepreneur   of Mihama
village.
        he inherited
        the estate on the hill.

        it became *Genyo-no Ie*
        (the *House of Genyo*)

And family reuniting some
years later,
        after the oldest
Genyo had   died.

His wife became
        Genyo-no Oba
widow of the benevolent
brother and landowner.

Okaasan and aunt cried for absent family.

*

a letter from
Japan.

told of
the loss of
    genyo-no ie.
  no more, no more,
  no more.

tears for a broken circle of family

genyo-no ie, the house of genyo,
mother's childhood –
    consumed in an act
  of purification.

but *Genyo-no oba* still wanders
along
      the night
corridors   hallways   empty rooms

of *Genyo*

they all wander:
the *oba*, my mother   my
father, sisters . . . brothers
Ojichan
    Obaachan

and my *Oniisan*
and
    maybe me, one day.

Ghost towns

Ghost town

dolphins
skitter   through
Venetian canals,

wolves roam
the
con-man's footprints of
Times Square,

and birds loosen & unfurl
their wings when
the industry clouds lift,
carried on the arms of the wind.

i feel the golden
wheat shafts as i dream
in the
fields of grief
in an empty town.

but
before patches of
        blue
come
    together
to create a new sky,

I wonder
if &   when
the plague
rain
              will subside
to be replaced   by
the storms
of cynicism, enmity, and
venality;

should i
just submit, just . . . succumb?

The Underground Rivers of Tokyo

Ukiyo-e

a floating
        world   above
the hidden river   flow
of
water to the sea.

I am changed and
stooped   but I
can
        hear the gurgling
of
pathways . beneath
my feet

and high above,
crows
        follow
    the paths of

the under

        -ground
    rivers

taking me away,
back
        to a time i
stood above a
river   an anonymous

river
        that flowed
    beneath my mother's
    japanese childhood

i watched the watercurrent
tumble
        over deep rocks and
    fish.

did my mother & her sisters play
in these waters?

giggling like
        girlish   liquid
into the air
surrounding me.

for some reason,
i slipped on smooth rock
and
            loose dirt

tumbling,
            turning,
blinded by sunlight,
anticipating the splash of
cool water
soaking
        through my shirt and
    shorts

my heavy shoes pulled me down

the surface was hard,

i sank   through
darkness without bottom

and opened
my mouth to drowning
water

but then a hand grabbed
my shoulder   another
wrapped
    around
  my chest

an assured grip, a strong grip

i was pulled up towards the sunlight.

my adult cousin
with the deformed right hand
had saved me.

I awake to tokyo crows
calling over-
                    head.
I want
        to return
to thank him, to celebrate
him.

  to think:

  he used to chase
  me around the farm-
  yard   his nub of a hand
  extended as a nightmare,

screaming laughter

I want to hold him as he
held me   soothe the pain of
his
        deformed
    appendage

but
concrete Edo sidewalks,
with layers of history
beneath

block
        my reach,
I pound and kick and hammer,
with bleeding   fists,

    I cannot reach,
    can't even see,
    the rivers that swell

with memory and past:

the paradise
        I seek is
    beyond   my grasp.

I can only listen to the
underground rivers and
wonder   with regret.

The lunar new year

the moon
    full, at its
  height,   sadly

begins to wane.

Why can't we
sit?
    in that bedazzled
  dining room,

at a large table in
Kwong Chow,
the fabled
Chinese restaurant with

a bar of Christmas lights
    and colour
television
elevated in the corner;
deeply lacquered
tables
      and chairs all
  around us, empty
  and waiting for
  tomorrow's patrons.

well after
midnight, after a gig,
chinatown
        the homeless apparitions
    wander   outside,

loose newspapers fly   like spirits
in the wind, garbage cans
topple, lids   clatter
to let me know they're there,

but the Cantonese *chow mein*
rests before us,
       steaming and
    shining;

Ted says to find the golden
morsels under-
neath with your chopsticks.   delicious and succulent.

the echo of telecasters
and Gibson guitars,
below -

  the growling Hammond B3 -
  rings in our ears,

Bill, stylish lead guitarist, smiles
in his chair, while
thunderous drums and thumping,
loping bass
             all underpin a skein of
    glorious
         harmony.

But we listen to   soft, gentle evening
music,
to talk about . . .

drink
      beer and wine
   and smoke
   the times away,

mrs. lumb smiles,
    with wide hips,
    battleship bosom,

her charm and eloquence exuding,
she
    plays the mother to us all

let the psychedelia pour onto the shiny wooden floor
to rise
    into the air
  on clouds
  of incense & empty vibrations.

why can't we?   one last time . . .
the   lunar new year
is about
    to shift
    and bill will be   gone

from his hospice bed,

yet I remain
to look on   high,
at the
    lunatic yellow moon
  and bask in

its sorrowful, lonely light.

why can't we?

for my friend bill lum and the Asia Minors

The Mourning of Empty Streets

Spectres writhing
above asphalt, crying out,
in
     grief

I see them
   I know them

but I can't recognize them.
I can't
       distinguish their
    identities

Spring

the cold mist
rises
    and settles among
new sprouts
the splattered rain distorts
the streets

Summer

the heat shimmer
off
   the roads
  where tracks have
  dug into the black-
  top

the bodies waver & disappear.

Fall

the
    autumn fog
  curls in
  off the lake

settles on the tongue
like tasteless candy
and friends
fade
  into dreams.

Winter

the winter steam
     of a killing
frost   above
a frozen
          pond on an
  early morning

hugging
       harbour
   shorelines,

creeping   along
hallowed ground settling
among
     gravestones

but
I can't separate them
from
     one another
the voices   all
meld into a choir
of
    the unknown.

yet they are
all
    my friends,
  my loves   my joy

and I think of them
until I stand in
the
    middle of a street
  and cry over memories

  out of sweet, sweet sorrow.

Night Rain

rain falls
    in a steady
  stream

a sweet, earthy
scent rises
as the   droplets
hit
    parched
  pavement

the petrichor:
the taste
    of acid
  rain.

the streets flood
    slowly
and
women   with umbrellas
and
    bare legs
step
    gingerly
  into the sparkling pools
  lying
    in the road

buildings glow,
their
    lights
   beckon in their
   shimmer

the promise of companionship,
family
   and maybe a communal meal
   prepared and served
   with
      love.

but the walls and roofs
are dark,
the windows black
with the wet growing and
spreading

no sign of warmth, meals, and loved ones.

during
these days of sickness
and
        stopped hearts

no lights shine,
not
        even streetlamps

no women
  with or without
umbrellas,
in
     the streets,

not even to perform
a *kabuki* drama.

only the moon
bright
            clouds
pulsate with
the storm from
above

nothing as lonely as
a
    rainy night,

washing away time and memories.

The Three Jewels

buddham saranam gacchami
dhammam saranam gacchami
sangham saranam gacchami

the recitation
    echoes in the strangely empty
  temple,
    rising to the rafters,

and escapes through the roof,
through to
        the ice-blue,
  clean air.

but the remnant sounds
resonate back to my
childhood   where
I am caught in a room
like
    this one, empty
  but steeped   in incense

and the words of the Buddha.

I am caught
in   the mystery
of
    the start of life
and the end of suffering –
the beginning of *Nirvana*.

I am caught . . .

for
    there is no end.

I have lived asking
the everlasting
question
    that everyone
    asks.   But there

is no answer . . . never an answer
so I grasp whatever community,
for *Sangha*,
there is;
like the   three jewels
of
    my youth

and cherish them until
they turn into ether.

I look to the Buddha for light
I look to the Dharma for wisdom
I look to the Sangha for comfort.

the three jewels
tarnish and sink into
a buried community

my endless search
for
    that which is lost.

the futility of desperation

Synaesthesia

Union of the senses

powell
       street
    is someone's
    memory

of an old Vancouver community,

but it has faded
to nearly
          nothing

it   did
       resurrect
    for a time

at dundas and spadina in Toronto,

powell &
    Jackson
    in Vancouver,

but only for a time.

1. New Year's Day – the Sight of Pain

furuya: mrs. & mr.
ishida   fishmongers to
the Toronto
       community.

oshogatsu   was the best
time
        at their house   with
  · a mountain range
   of cooked shrimp greedily
   consumed

by the Yoshida brothers and cousins   good
Buddhist boys

gluttonous slobber,

the slurp
            of seajuice,
      a mountain
      of   shells, abdomens &
              heads

mr. ishida   perched
on his
        easy chair

   paralysed by a stroke,
   he drooled and the
   waterfall mucus   dripped
   off
        his chin into   his lap
   where his dead hand
   rested   palm up, fingers
   crook'd and   pleading.

his fingers   that
pulled
         back
   the fresh flesh
   of *maguro*,
               sake and
      butter-
         fish

the fingers   that
picked at
the tiny white, translucent
bones   that
may have stuck to
the roof of the mouth
are
      withered and
      gnarled   tortured   twisted

                  archi-

tecturally unsound.

he couldn't even
cry   to his wife,
son and
        daughters.

his face a mask of pain –
        frozen
        horror.

yet the revellers
        welcomed
the New Year   with *osechi ryori*:
decorative *ebi* for   long life   strands of *gobo*
for good luck and stability   and *kazunoko
kombu*
        for prosperity   fertility.

Prosperity frozen by a stroke,
but
        the silence, the peace
        of his mask,
        is
            the centre of the
        New Year.

2. the Touch of Appetite

before
        furuya   there was
the continental family co-op-
erative
        founded by
kagetsu, shin, mori

and kozai *sensei*   for the Buddhist
Church & Community   and

nikko gardens   a fancy jpze restaurant
owned by   the kadonaga bros.
who
        hated one another
    for some reason –
    long lost

gus and   jim:
so much so   one stayed in front as the host
the other in the back supervising the cooking

can't remember which,
a façade of a family

shrimp *tempura*
golden
                crispy,
    teishoku   with
    chow mein, gohan
    kinpira gobo

and *chawan-mushi*   a specialty.

Sukiyaki   the song playing
in
        the background

[just the voice, no mask of recognition]

the lilt of Japanese melody
the sense of the familiar
and   comfort

uncle eizo
peeled off several   bills
to pay for aunt sally's
celebratory meal.

I was impressed   *they are rich.*

and
        the ginza
restaurant   a cosy
café   with a long counter
and red vinyl stools;
tables
        lined the wall,
near dundas and
bay   *ochazuke*   a specialty

with *denbasuke* (New Denver
born
                and made)
and *karashina*
right out of the backyard garden
as
    tsukemono.

Dundas
        Union
the shelves lined &
groaned with   cans/tins/bottles of
    mysterious
  food   from Japan.

ryoji-*san*
　　　　　his hang-dog face
　　wondering what i

wanted, trying to remember
my name

his driver/partner
restocking　　the van
with
　　　tofu, fish (fresh and dried),
　　packaged *sembei*　　and
　　rice - 100 pounds of, 50 pounds of,
　　20 . . .

a route of jpze cdn homes
including ours on
lvy
　　　Avenue,
dad or l carrying
the 100 lbs into the basement
　　poured the *kome* into
tin cans
　　　　　so the mice didn't feast

my exercise to prove my strength

he never missed mrs.miyamoto
at 91 lvy
　　　she was the community
　　caterer　　always old, always loud
　　always darkskinned　　always
　　friendly　　always good food.

98

my appetite touched with sadness.
the store
        (long gone,
    long . . .
)

3. The Scent of Friendship

the girls
        came by once in a while,
    i never knew when

but   i enjoyed their company:

Janice was my age   more tomboy
than anything   long hair
and short skirt   ready for a fight,
but we never did

Aimee   was the pretty one,
smart
        and demure,
    short hair and always
    with a smile

i always closed my eyes
in the swirl of their
perfume

early days   we
played hide-and-go-
seek   in my house.

i once found   Janice
under the bed

her face concealed
behind the   headboard,   her legs
spread wide-open   the thighs singing with
careless smoothness
              and her white
      panties   gleaming
      with
          intrigue

the disembodied returns
in
          dreams

never could find Aimee,
probably kid stuff
to
      her

their visits were never long enough,
and when we grew up   and i
visited their
narrow house on dundas near
spadina

          one of the last to live in j-town,
          Sugimoto-*san's* Danforth Cleaners
          was an anomaly

i could touch

      the two walls of their rowhouse
      just by standing in the middle

of the livingroom and stretching
my arms out

perhaps a false memory

the last i saw them, their parents
had decided to move
to the suburbs   relocating the
business to   Danforth Rd.
appropriately enough.

we didn't play hide-and-go-seek,
we sat down to
            cookies and tea.
        we were at university after all

and we said goodbye
in
        our masquerade of friendship

i hear Aimee
married a *Sansei* guy
and collects
classical   albums

don't know what happened
to   Janice but   i will
            always   know
        her perfume, as it was

the last day,
she kissed   me   goodbye.

her perfume the scent of a mask

4. The Loud Presence of Community

odori   at *obon*
women & girls in *kimono*
in *zori*   with fans, parasols
and
     clackers
with masks of happiness
and makeup.
they circle the *yagura*
singer on top, *taiko* in front

and they begin to move   a wheel
set
     in motion
the wheel of *karma*

the hep guys and gals
jive   and swing to
          the J-Cats
the swells & debs
in smooth suits
          and dresses

the legion hall came alive
to *Nisei* romance

and the *Sansei*
rock out   /
   dance   to the Asia Minors,
to 3-minute pop records on the
turntable.

at the   Church,
basement hall
        in miniskirts and
platform shoes

ah, a joyous noise,
the   faceless
            joy of community.

5. The Taste of Waves

powell
        street
    is someone's
    idea of a dream,

of a community.

the pacific ocean's cry
speaks
        in waves
        sad for the
        disappeared

sad for the voices empty
of words
        of sighs
        of sound.

but upon awakening,
the sea
     evaporates,
condenses   and

falls
     as rain – as with
   memory.

on Toronto streets,
there are
calls for one last festival.

but only a mask
mouths
    a soundless
   answer.

Crows in the Moonlight

The Black Crows of Hokkaido

crows, black and large,
sit
   like lumps of coal,
  glistening and hard,

as they occupy
the
streets of Sapporo.

they confer; they argue;
they
      complain.

they plot murder . . .

and I walk around them
cautiously
     slowly   so
as not to disturb.

they look evil
if
    ever   evil
  showed itself.

are there four?
    please,
  so I'll be wealthy . . .

no, five.

my legs cramp,
a cough grows
stronger . . .

I can't taste,
        I can't smell
    the pain of old
    age.

six?
what will they take?
my   wallet   my father's
watch?

my health?
        my life

seven?
but I'm here in Japan.

no, there are 8 . . . no 5 . . . no . . .
it is
    the time of 5 crows.

for whom should I weep,

    for
        whom
    shall I grieve?

who . . . the loss . . . ?
the lost?

*The crow in Japan is evidence of divine intervention. They tell of changes in
life. Four crows bring wealth. Five predict disease and pain. Six denote loss*

through theft. Seven crows mean a change of place. Eight symbolize grief and sorrow. The crow-god is seen as representing guidance; hence, the crow points to the magic and mystery within life.

Starry Night

the august stars
      spark like
  fire that dances
  in

the night   all around.

Bach plays in
the background
as
     music always does.

and I gaze in wonder
as
     she lies before me

sky black, absence of blue,
a great
     dome
   in motion

portrait of a dreaming mind

the red soil
beneath
   her bare feet
the aches
& pains released
their
   hold and she
rises to the distance
to meet once again

her
        father, mother, grand-
parents, aunts   uncles

        and ancestors she never
        knew

and they smile as she smiles;
such
        happens on a
starry night during *Obon*

Self-portrait in the gallery of the self

and the swirls
      carry over to the
next painting

Edith Piaf
sings
from another era

plaintive   blue
French blues
        in the smoke
   of a
   café   sipping absinthe
   talking about God and
   love

can He hear
from
      so far away?

my self-portrait
swirls   and
        turns on
its axis

grinding into my mind.

So much pain, so much anguish, so
much self-loathing
long
        in my past

gone now
that
        I am alone.

Crows above
            the fields
    of my
            evaporated
        past.

Edith Piaf
    continues to sing
in the dark yellow
day
as I labour
in
        the fields of wheat

crows
are flying aBOVE
telling
    me what to do.

i
    revel in
  the globs of umber

the blue with
shades
    of white   as
Edith stops . . .

telling me what to do.

The Crows of Wonder

the crows of wonder
tell
    me of my love

the crows of magic
speak
of my fate

the crows of
music
      sing
  of time and
  an ending

trees sweat
in the heat, birds
chirp
      a complaint
and
   the ground
  swells   with infection,

during
this august time
of death and
    commemoration,
    veneration . . . consecration.

The Crow Moon

a full moon
        in March,
    the last of the winter.

a Crow Moon,
when the calling
of
crows signals
the end of   snow,
ice and bitter   wind,

when warm winds
caress   the land,
coaxing
            it back to life.

        and flowers, mouths open, reach
        for the sun and rain
        and trees turn green & sway   to
        watch
                over.

so say our brethren of the land.

but
the cold remains in pools
around plant shoots

I do hear the cawing,
the crying
        of winter's   end,
for the beginning of

spring

I too call to the moon
to shine
a warm light   the end of
death

to bring about
rebirth   and renewal

Crow Moon   bright
and demure,

sing to me   sing
of
wealth   sing a
song of   health
and of
        my own self.

The Mask

shadows
    cover the
  darkness   of night:

my father's mask;
my
        okaasan's mask;
hideki's mask;

    the masks of
    mike, jim and   bill.

cool mike,
    celestial jim,
  stylish bill

their masks hide their lives

and there is the one
mask
    of pain, grief,
  and loss

    that hides
    from
        all of us:

the mask of the pandemic;
the mask
    of disease . . .

Acknowledgements

Visions of Chisato published in Vallum Magazine, Issue 19.2 2022.
Masks, poem placed third for the Nick Blatchford Occasional Verse Prize. Contest sponsored by the *New Quarterly.* Aug. 26 Published in Issue 160, The New Quarterly November 2021
Poem *Haunted by the Immaterial World* published in *Beliveau Review,* Volume 2, No. 4, Issue 7. Stratford ON. May 2021
Poem, *Ghost Town,* selected for *We are One: Poems from the Pandemic,* an anthology for Bayeux Arts Publishers. November 2020.

Illustration, *Crows in the Moonlight after Ogata Kōrin'* [1658–1716], an early woodblock print by Sakai Hōitsu (1761-1828), a Japanese painter of the Rinpa school. Image courtesy of the Princeton University Art Museum.

A great debt of gratitude to Nurjehan Aziz, MG Vassanji, Sabrina Pignataro and all the people at Mawenzi House Publishers.

Glossary

Awa Odori	Idiot's dance
Bonsan	Buddhist priest
Chawan mushi	steamed egg custard
Ebi	shrimp
Denbasuke	pickled radish, originated in New Denver BC
Fue	Japanese wooden flute
Furuya	grocery store at Dundas and Huron Streets in Toronto
Genyo-no oba	Genyo (estate and name of my aunt) elderly woman
Gobo	burdock root
Gohan	steamed rice
Hannya	female demon, noh theatre
Heart Sutra	set of aphorisms expressing the perfection of wisdom x
Ie	house
Karashina	mustard greens
Katana	Japanese sword
Kazunoko kombu	herring eggs on seaweed
Kinpira gobo	braised burdock root
Kitsune	supernatural fox
Kome	uncooked rice
Maguro	tuna
Nisei	second generation Japanese Canadians (first born in Canada)
Noh	classical Japanese theatre
Oba, Obaachan	aunt
Obon	Buddhist Festival of the Dead
Ochazuke	cold rice covered with green tea, pickles accompaniment
Odori	folk dance

Ofuro	bath
Ojiichan	grandfather
Okaa, Okaachan, Okaasan	Mother
Oni	devil, demon
Oniisan	eldest brother
Osechi ryori	traditional New Year's delicacies
Oshogatsu	New Year's Day
Sake	salmon
Sansei	third generation Japanese Canadians
Seiza	meditation
Sembei	rice crackers
Shoji	paper walls
Sutra	chants to the Buddha
Taiko	Japanese drum
Tanko Bushi	Coalminer's Dance
Tatami	straw mat flooring
Teishoku	Japanese meal set
Tengu	mischievous supernatural being
Tsukemono	pickled vegetables
ue o muite arukō	*I walk with my eyes looking upward* Japanese title of the hit song Sukiyaki, sung by Kyu Sakamoto 1962
Ukiyo-e	woodblock print
Yagura	drum and singer tower for Obon
Yomesan	bride, young woman
Zori	straw sandals